100 QUESTIONS THAT NON-MEMBERS ASK ABOUT UNITARIAN UNIVERSALISM

BY JOHN SIAS

From interviews with Rev. Steve Edington

TRANSITION PUBLISHING
Nashua, New Hampshire

First printing September, 1994
Second printing May, 1995
Third printing November, 1995
Second edition November, 1996
Third edition March, 1998
Fourth edition April, 1999
Fifth edition December, 2000
Sixth edition September, 2002
Seventh edition April, 2005
Eighth edition April, 2007

Printed in the United States of America

Designed by Jill Shaffer

Additional copies are available from:
  Unitarian Universalist Church
  58 Lowell Street
  Nashua, NH 03064
  603-882-1091
  office-admin@uunashua.org

ISBN 0-9654497-3-4

PREFACE

A few years ago I learned that in this nation of 300 million people, there are fewer than 200,000 Unitarian Universalists.

I wondered, "Are UUs so rare because people have studied the religion and rejected it? Or is it that so few people are even acquainted with the religion?"

Believing that the latter situation might be the case; I began to assemble questions about Unitarian Universalism, obtaining them from a variety of people outside the religion: Catholics, Protestants, Jews and fundamentalists. I even went inside the religion, seeking questions from both present and former church members and ministers.

Rev. Steve Edington of the Nashua, New Hampshire UU Church is the source of most of the answers. If you don't like the response to a particular question, I'll tell you that Steve didn't answer that one, or Steve did answer it but I didn't write what he told me. Otherwise he would be the author and I wouldn't have had anything to do. The answers do not represent the views of all Unitarian Universalists—there is great diversity among individual UU churches and ministers. But leaving room for our differences, we think the answers given here are fairly representative.

To publisher Bud Swanson, president of Transition Publishing, who gave this little book soul and character, thank you.

Nine printings and 25,000 books later, we seem to be holding our own. Most important, many people have told us that 100 Questions has helped them decide to become a UU.

John Sias
April, 2007

CONTENTS

1 BELIEFS, CREEDS AND DOCTRINES

Come return to your place in the pews,
And hear our heretical views:
You were not born in sin
So lift up your chin,
You have only your dogmas to lose.

LEONARD MASON, UU MINISTER

What do Unitarian Universalists believe?

- Every individual should be encouraged to develop a personal philosophy of life.
- Everyone is capable of reasoning.
- We do not need any other person, official or organization to tell us what to believe.
- We should be able to present religious opinions openly, without fear of censure or reprisal.
- All people should be tolerant of the religious ideas of others.
- Truth is not absolute; it changes over time.
- Everyone should continue to search for the truth.
- Everyone has an equal claim to life, liberty and justice.
- People should govern themselves by democratic processes.
- Ideas should be open to criticism.
- Good works are the natural product of a good faith.

Which values do you hold highest?

We regard the highest values to be integrity, caring, compassion, social justice, truth, personal peace and harmony. Advancing these values is a major purpose of our congregations.

Does the UUA have a creed?

No. Although the bylaws of the association do contain a section on purposes and principles, it is not a statement of a religious creed.

Do you subscribe to any doctrines?

We have no specific doctrines to which members are expected to subscribe. However, the bylaws of the UUA (Unitarian Universalist Association) and member churches and societies do contain a Statement of Purpose and Principles (see page 18). These are the basis of a solemn agreement that member churches will support the UUA and that the UUA will support the individual churches.

What do you NOT believe?

We do not believe that any religious precept or doctrine must be accepted as true simply because some religious organization, tradition or authority says it is. Neither do we believe that all UUs should have identical beliefs.

Do some UUs have different beliefs than other UUs?

They certainly do. Since individual freedom of belief is one of our basic principles, it follows that there will be differing beliefs among us. Found in today's churches are humanism, agnosticism, atheism, theism, liberal Christianity, neo-paganism and earth spiritualism. These beliefs are not mutually exclusive—it's possible to hold more than one. While we are bound by a set of common principles, we leave it to the individual to decide what particular beliefs lead to those principles.

Do you believe in God?

While there is a perception of UUs that we do not believe in God, it is much more accurate to say that we do not have a single, defined concept of God in which all UUs are expected to believe. Each member is free to explore and develop an understanding of God that is meaningful to him or her. They're also free to reject the term or concept altogether.

Most of us do not believe in a supernatural, supreme being who can directly intervene in and alter human life or the mechanism of the natural world. Many believe in a spirit of life or a power within themselves, which some choose to call God.

Do you believe in a personal God?

A personal God is one with whom someone feels a one-to-one relationship, a deity who cares specifically for that individual and to whom that person can appeal directly. Few UUs would characterize God in such personal terms.

What role does God play in the Church?

The extent to which you will hear God mentioned in a Sunday service will vary from church to church. In most services, the emphasis is on those issues of human growth, human potential and personal human issues that we all face in day-to-day living. There is also an emphasis on social, moral and ethical issues that confront us. Although subjects are presented from the religious perspective of the minister or the speaker, it is never assumed that all present have a common understanding of God.

God means different things to different UUs. To some, the term has little or no meaning. Most UUs would disavow the idea of God as a Supernatural Supreme Being. However, the idea of "God" as a Sacred Presence, or Life Spirit, within the natural world and universe, does have resonance with a good number of Unitarian Universalists.

Whatever the case may be, we offer an accepting congregation where each person can discover what gives his or her life meaning, purpose and value.

Do you believe in the existence of spiritual beings?

Not in the sense of something that is disembodied. Most agree that there is a spiritual dimension to life that is connected to the physical, mental, emotional, and psychological aspects of life.

Do you believe in miracles?

We do not believe in miracles in any supernatural way since our ideas of God generally do not include a deity who has the ability to alter the workings of the natural world. Most UUs feel that the gift of life itself is sufficient miracle, and that we should live as fully, joyfully and responsibly as we can.

Do you believe in Jesus?

We do not believe that Jesus Christ was born of a virgin, performed miracles and was resurrected from death. We do admire and respect the way he lived, the power of his love, the force of his example, and his values.

Most UUs regard Jesus as one of several important moral and ethical teachers who have shown humans how to live a life of love, service and compassion. Though some of us may question whether Jesus was an actual historical figure, we believe his teachings are of significant moral value.

How do you regard the Bible?

We regard the Bible as one of many important religious texts but do not consider it unique or exclusive in any way. We do not interpret it literally. We think some parts of it offer more truth and relevance than other parts. Although UUs respect the Bible and regard some of its content as great literature, it is not a central document in our religion.

Do you believe in life after death?

Very few UUs believe in a continuing, individualized existence after physical death. Even fewer believe in the physical existence of places called heaven or hell where one goes after dying. We believe immortality manifests itself in the lives of those we affect during our lifetime and in the legacy we leave when we die.

Do you believe in the concept of evolution?

Yes. We believe that more complex life forms have evolved from less complex life forms.

What are the bonds that unify UUs?

While there are no written or verbal doctrines designed for that purpose, we have both stated and unstated bonds which unify us. The stated bonds are the Principles and Purposes of the UUA which we support individually and collectively.

Among the unstated bonds are our mutual respect for each other and our appreciation of the many religious, philosophical and spiritual paths which our members pursue. We are bound together in our mutual concern for one another's well being, and our willingness to aid each other in time of need.

2 DEFINITIONS AND DIFFERENCES

What is a favorite UU bumper sticker?
"To question is the answer!"

How do you think most churches would define a Christian?

Classical Christian doctrine would describe a Christian as a person who believes:

- that God, the Ultimate, the Divine (call it what one wishes) was uniquely revealed to humans in the person of Jesus of Nazareth, also called Jesus the Christ.
- that Jesus was God on Earth, who came to save human beings from the state of sin into which they were born (Original Sin) by his death on the cross (the Atonement), and then triumphed over death (the Resurrection). In response to this act of God, humans are to give thanks to Him, accept Jesus as their Savior and dedicate their life to Jesus by following his teachings and example.
- that miracles can happen through a supernatural deity who can alter the workings of the natural world.

For Protestants, the authority for their religion is the Bible. For Catholics the authority is the teachings of the Catholic Church.

Liberal Christianity (from which the Unitarians and the Universalists evolved) either downplays or dismisses the idea of Original Sin, and sees Jesus as one sent from God to show us how to live better lives. Liberal Christians view God as a force for good rather than a supernatural being. They are more flexible in their interpretation of Scripture, reading it more in its historic context and giving symbolic rather than literal interpretation to many passages.

Are UUs Christian?

Although Unitarianism and Universalism at one time were liberal Protestant Christian denominations, both drew away from their Christian heritage to embrace the principle of individual freedom of belief. While some congregations have retained a liberal Christian identity, today only about 20% of UUs would call themselves Christian.

How do you differ from Christians?

A primary way we differ is that we do not regard Jesus as a unique revelation of God. Most UUs (even UU Christians) would reject a literal interpretation of accepted Christian beliefs such as the Virgin Birth, the miracles of Jesus and the physical Resurrection of Christ. While UU Christians would accept a symbolic interpretation of these events, most UUs view Jesus as one of a number of great moral and ethical teachers who have lived on earth.

What do UUs and humanists have in common?

Because ours is a very humanistically-oriented religion, most UUs regard themselves as humanists in one sense or another. But, like the term God, humanism also means different things to different UUs.

Basically, humanism means that we humans are responsible for our destiny for better or worse and we cannot rely on an outside power or deity to determine our individual or collective fate. Humanism is also an affirmation of the power of the human mind and the human spirit.

There are both secular and religious humanists. Secular humanists do not believe in any kind of deity; they find little, if any, value in religious language, stories, myths or symbols of any religious tradition.

The religious humanist, while holding to the above definition of humanism, does not completely disavow the idea of God. Usually defining God as a power deep within themselves, they also find certain messages or themes in religious stories that provide them with understanding and guidelines for human living.

There are both secular and religious humanists within our church family, and we make room for both.

What is the difference between a Unitarian and a Universalist?

From an institutional perspective there has been no difference since 1961 when the Unitarians and Universalists merged.

What might be considered the watch words of Unitarian Universalism?

Traditionally they have been freedom, reason and tolerance. While today's UUs still revere these three words, they have added three more words: spirit, grace and love.

What are some characteristics of UUs?

The typical UU is well-educated, moderately affluent, and professionally employed. Most of our local churches are working hard to attract a more diverse membership. We want to be welcoming congregations, free of economic, religious, racial, ethnic, or sexual discrimination.

Is Unitarian Universalism really a religion?

In dealing with beliefs and theology, it's important to note that Unitarian Universalism is a way of being religious rather than a religious doctrine. For us, religion is an ongoing search for meaning, purpose, value and spiritual depth in one's life. We believe that individuals are entitled to make their own search, and that not all persons (not even all UUs) are going to share the same beliefs.

Ours is a non-creedal, non-doctrinal religion which affirms the individual's freedom of belief. For this reason it is not possible to give a blanket answer to whether or not UUs believe in God, Jesus, the Bible or life after death. Although we do not all believe the same thing about these and other matters, we do believe that each person has the integrity and the ability to come to terms with their religious beliefs in a way that is right for that person.

Rev. F. Forrester Church has defined religion as, "Our human response to the dual reality of being alive and knowing we will die." This captures a common UU understanding of religion. It is how we respond to life, and how we find meaning, purpose and depth in life, in the face of our human mortality.

What is your attitude toward other religious faiths such as Judaism, Hinduism and Buddhism?

We believe there is wisdom in most, if not all, of the world's religions. We feel each is valuable for what it can tell us about ourselves and our world, and how its members find religious meaning and direction.

Do UUs believe in a universal religion?

We believe in the universality of religion in that we recognize all humans ask questions such as "Why am I here? What is the meaning and purpose of my life? Why do I have to die?" Realizing all religions seek to provide answers to questions like these, we think there is much wisdom in their many answers.

Few UUs contend that there is, or ever will be, a single universal religion that is right for everyone.

3 LIFE, DEATH, SALVATION, SIN

A Universalist minister of an obstreperous congregation became annoyed at the infighting during a meeting of the board. Interrupting them, he asked the board members what Universalism meant to them. On this one thing, they agreed, "Universalism means universal salvation; all of us are going to heaven when we die."

The minister said, "You know, if I were God, I'd put you guys in mansions right next to each other and make you live together for a million years or so until you learned to get along with each other."

How do you regard death and how does this affect the way you live?

Most UUs regard death as the final and total end of our existence. Rather than seeing this in a morbid or despairing sense, we view the finality of death as a compelling reason to live life as fully as possible.

Although we regard death as the end of our conscious life, we hope that we will live on in the minds and hearts of those persons whose lives we enriched during our lives.

How do you regard sin?

We do not believe that a person is born and enslaved in the manner that the doctrine of Original Sin teaches.

We believe that people are punished by their sins, not for them, and that the evil people do lives with them. We also believe that we are enriched by our virtues and that the good we do lives with us and helps make the world better.

You could attend a UU church for years and seldom hear the word sin. For most UUs, sin really means being separated from our better selves. It is seen more as a condition we need to correct than "bad deeds" done.

How do you explain evil?

We have no quick doctrine-based answers to explain evil, pain and suffering, and the fact that life can be hellish at times. For all our optimism, most of us acknowledge there is a broken, fragmented or fallen side to humanity, and in each of our lives. While we admit the existence of this negative side of life, we try not to give in to it.

You will find many UUs involved in efforts to make this a more just, peaceful, sane and livable world at local, national and global levels. We strive to act and think in ways that will allow all humans to reach their potential.

And even if we cannot explain why people suffer, we can try to help them when they do.

Can UUs go to heaven or hell?

Since there is no way to know for sure if we go any place when we die, very few, if any of us believe in the physical existence of a place called heaven or hell.

What about salvation? Can a UU be saved?

Salvation is not a word we use frequently.

We do not believe people are born into a state of sin from which they must be saved in order to avoid spending an eternity suffering in hell.

Since we believe in neither original sin nor hell, we do not feel a need to be saved from either.

When we do use the term "salvation" it refers to a sense of personal wholeness or fulfillment, or being at peace with oneself.

Do you believe in a Redeemer?

No. We believe we should be judged by how well we live our lives and serve others, not in what a redeemer will do for us. We respect religious and spiritual leaders such as Jesus, Moses and Buddha for what they can teach us about living, not as redeemers in the traditional sense.

If you do not fear God, hell, or eternal damnation, what is your incentive to act morally and responsibly?

We feel that people who live moral and ethical lives usually do so because they have a sense of responsibility to themselves and to others. Our incentive is that we want to live in a more sane, peaceful, and just world than the one we have at present, and we wish to pass on a better world to succeeding generations.

To hold that moral and ethical living only occurs because people fear hell or damnation is to demean those who seek to lead morally and ethically responsible lives.

ATTITUDES AND INTERESTS

A little woman of middle years requested the clerk to cut 40 yards of pink chiffon for her. When he asked her what she could possibly want with 40 yards of chiffon, she explained, "I'm making a nightie for myself."

"But surely you don't need 40 yards. You are not a large woman."

"Yes, but my husband is a Unitarian and he'd much rather look for something than actually find it."

What is the your attitude toward women and minorities?

Although it's a matter of opinion whether men and women have achieved complete equality in our religion, feminist theology has had a strong and positive impact on our churches, particularly in the last decade.

However, our record on attracting racial, cultural and ethnic minorities into our denomination is not nearly as good. We are working hard to break out of our traditional mold to include a more diverse membership.

Would you categorize UUs as optimistic or pessimistic?

In spite of the weakness and frailty of all humans, we are optimistic about the potential of all persons.

*Do you believe Unitarian Universalism
is the only true religion?*

No. We believe that every religion contains truths about who we are, why we are here and how we ought to live with ourselves and others.

*How would you characterize
your religion?*

Not only do we have a hopeful and optimistic attitude about life, we believe strongly that humans have great potential to recognize right, correct wrongs, find solutions and make this a better world. Rather than feel bound by human weaknesses and frailties, we emphasize human strengths. We believe people have the strength, power and intelligence to make good things happen. You might call it a "can do" religion.

*How do you explain
why bad things happen?*

We have no religion-based explanation of life's tragedies, horrors and heartbreaks. Life can be senselessly lost, diminished and demeaned in many ways but most UUs do not attribute these losses to the will of God. Instead, most UUs agree we live in an indifferent universe.

Rather than try to explain life's inexplicable tragedies, we try to help people when such tragedies strike, and do all we can to restore them to hope again.

*Where do you turn when
you need support?*

Most turn to family, friends, and people within their religious community with whom they are especially close and whom they rely on. Some UUs do feel a relationship with a power greater than themselves and to whom they will turn when they need support. They give this power many names. God is one of them, but far from the only one.

Are fears or threats part of your religion?

No, certainly not in the sense of divine punishment for a person's mistakes. We believe that human beings should be accountable for their actions and make amends for any harm they may bring to others. But we don't believe that God will punish them.

What role does science play in your church?

We accept the teachings of science and the scientific method. UUs believe that the scientific principle that states there is always more truth to be discovered about our world, also applies to religion.

5 HISTORY

During a staff meeting of the UUA, the president was holding forth in his usual windy and repetitive manner. A staff member who had been raised with the Bible, slipped a note to a colleague with a similar background. The note said, "Hebrews 13:8."

His colleague burst into laughter, recalling the passage, "Jesus Christ, the same yesterday, today and forever."

Is Unitarianism Universalism an American religion?

Its origins are in Europe and the Protestant Reformation. However, contemporary Unitarian Universalism is an American religion which took root and flourished in New England in 1750-1800 as a liberal spin-off from the Congregational Church.

What is the history of Unitarian Universalism?

While both Unitarianism and Universalism grew out of the left wing of the Protestant Reformation in Europe during the 16th century, both took on an American flavor when they were introduced in the United States. Both religions originated in part as a protest against two Calvinist doctrines: total depravity (Original Sin) and Predestination (the doctrine

15

of the elect—the belief that God has determined whether you will go to Heaven even before you were born).

The Unitarians, while recognizing the reality of evil, did not believe that any person was born in a state of total corruption from which they could be rescued solely at the whim of an arbitrary God. They believed that all people had the potential for good or evil depending upon both the life they chose to live and upon the social environment in which they were born and raised.

The Unitarians were Christians who believed that people should interpret the Bible in the light of human reason. Although Jesus and the Bible were central to their faith, they regarded Jesus as more of a moral and ethical teacher than a supernatural being. They did believe in the divinity of Jesus, that he was the son of God but not the same as God. The term "Unitarian" originally meant "non-trinitarian" a belief in one unified God rather than a three-part entity.

The term Universalism originally meant that every person could be saved (universal salvation) as opposed to the salvation of a few whom God would select to save. Although Christian, the Universalists did not believe a loving God would condemn people to an eternity of hell. They believed that the souls of all dead people would eventually be reconciled to this loving God, although it would take a longer time for some to get to heaven than others.

Both groups had their American origins in the late 18th century. Unitarian and Universalist churches were established mostly in New England but during the 19th century, Unitarianism spread west and many churches were organized in California.

Throughout the 19th and into the early 20th centuries, Unitarianism and Universalism were liberal Christian alternatives to the more harsh and dogmatic forms of Christianity of that time. During the 20th century, both religions began to move away from their Christian origin toward a religion based on individual freedom of belief. The Universalists retained their Christian identity longer than the Unitarians.

In today's congregation, it's common to find a variety of beliefs: humanist, agnostic, theist, atheist, liberal Christian, etc. Over the past decade, feminist theology has made an impact: our hymn books are gender inclusive, and half our seminary students are women.

The term Unitarian affirms that we believe there is a unity of all life, what the UUA Principles and Purposes calls "the interdependent web of all existence of which we are a part." The term Universalism indicates universality of religion itself. In the UUA Principles and Purposes, we affirm that you can find wisdom in all the world's religions.

When did the merger of Unitarianism and Universalism take place?

The difference between the two movements ran much more along class and cultural lines than theological ones. The Unitarians originally attracted white collar people: professionals, educators, cultural leaders, etc. The Universalist congregations were comprised mostly of blue collar working class people such as farmers and fishermen.

By the middle of the 20th century, these distinctions had blurred, making a merger both possible and financially necessary for the survival of the two religions. After several years of discussion and negotiation during the 1950s, the Unitarian Universalist Association (UUA) was formed in 1961.

How is Unitarian Universalism distinctive from other religions?

We have no religious creed nor do we require members to adhere to any doctrines. A religion based on individual freedom of belief, we encourage all members to pursue their own religious and spiritual journeys.

6 THE UNITARIAN UNIVERSALIST ASSOCIATION

In 1993, the UUA General Assembly celebrated 200 years of Universalism in America. One of the old-time Universalists who hadn't been happy with the merger said, "You know, there never was a real merger with Unitarianism. Actually, the Unitarians gobbled up the Universalists." Thinking aloud, he added, "But I guess it's really no problem, since you are what you eat!"

What world-wide goals and values does the Unitarian Universalist Association promote in its Statement of Purpose and Principles?

- Every person is worthy and should be treated with dignity.
- People should treat each other with justice, equality and compassion.
- We should accept the differences that tend to separate us.
- Everyone should have the freedom and responsibility to search for the truth.
- We should strive to use democratic processes both within UU congregations and the world at large.
- We should work for peace, liberty and justice for everyone.
- We should acknowledge and respect how interdependent every one of us is.

Where are the headquarters of the UUA?

The Association's headquarters are at 25 Beacon Street in Boston. We elect a full-time president every four years who manages the organization and represents it in the religious and secular world. Each June, delegates from congregations throughout the nation meet in a five-day General Assembly to hear reports, elect officers and take positions on public issues.

There are approximately 1,056 congregations in North America (and a few in other parts of the world) who are affiliated with the UUA. Compared to most mainline Protestant denominations, we are quite small. However, we have enjoyed a slow but steady growth since the late 1970s.

How is the president of the UUA selected?

Every four years at the UU General Assembly, the delegates and recognized proxies elect a president, who probably began campaigning 18 months earlier for the full-time office. If eligible for reelection, the president usually runs unopposed for one additional four-year term.

7 CUSTOMS, CEREMONIES, CELEBRATIONS

A young man who came into unexpected wealth immediately fulfilled his long-held fantasy, and bought himself a Ferrari. So enamored of the car was he that he sought to have it religiously blessed.

However, every priest, rabbi and minister he approached was offended at the idea of offering a blessing over an expensive automobile, but one suggested he contact a UU minister, figuring they were open to such things.

Approaching the minister, the young man asked, "Can you give a blessing for my Ferrari?"

The minister replied, "I guess I can, but I have one question."

"What's that?"

The minister asked, "What's a blessing?"

Is ceremony part of your tradition?

Birth, marriage, death — we mark all of these occasions with ceremony. These ceremonies are not considered sacraments. The minister tailors each service to the people personally involved, so that the ceremony will be especially appropriate to them.

Do you have a baptism ceremony?

We have a Dedication and Naming ceremony performed at the same age that children in other religions are baptized or christened. The parents and sponsors (or godparents) promise to provide the child a healthful upbringing — physically, emotionally, mentally and spiritually. Water is often used (a few drops on the child's head) as a symbol of the renewal and regeneration of life, which the child represents so well.

Is there an induction ceremony for new members?

The type of ceremony varies by congregation; there is no officially sanctioned induction ceremony. Two or three times each year, many congregations conduct an informal ceremony as part of a Sunday service in which new members are formally welcomed to the church.

Do UUs celebrate Christmas and Easter?

Yes, we do. The difference may be that we tie these holidays more to the changing seasons than we do to traditional Christian themes. They are honored as celebrations of the winter solstice and the spring equinox — the hope and promise symbolized by the lengthening of the daylight hours in December, and the renewal of life in spring after the winter season of darkness.

The traditional accounts of the birth of Jesus and of the Resurrection are sometimes included in these celebrations and cited as myths which contain a positive message about human life. The birth of a child, for example, represents the hope and promise found in each new life. The crucifixion and Resurrection are symbolic of how new life can emerge even after a time of pain and suffering. As with the Bible itself, these stories are not taken literally but for what they symbolically tell us about human life.

We celebrate Easter as the return of spring and the renewal of life; in this respect we draw more on the pagan rather than the Christian origin of this holiday. The New Testament accounts of the Resurrection may be cited as a symbol of the strength, power and renewal of life. We do not accept the idea of a physical resurrection.

Most UUs regard Jesus as one of a number of especially gifted, insightful teachers of humanity. These leaders have emerged over the course of history to teach us how we should live and be at peace with ourselves and each other. Jesus is not considered unique in this respect.

His death reflects a tragic and painful end of life. Because UUs have long rejected the idea of Original Sin, the belief that Jesus atoned for the sins of the world by his death has little relevance for us. Even when

Unitarianism and Universalism were clearly Christian faiths, they still rejected this doctrine of atonement.

Do you accept cremation?

We view cremation as an accepted form of burial and it is widely chosen by UUs.

Do you pray during the service, and if so, to whom?

This varies by congregation. Most Sunday services have a time for meditation, often preceded by spoken words from the minister. In a theistic congregation, prayers will be addressed to a deity; in a humanist congregation, prayers will take the form of personal reflection and meditation.

Do you pray at home?

It is entirely up to the individual. Although more UUs are seeking ways to cultivate a spiritual life, few would characterize prayer as a personal relationship with a Supreme Being.

Prayer for UUs is a way of getting in touch with one's self.

Do UUs participate in prescribed rites and sacraments such as the Lord's Supper, confirmation, confession and last rites?

No. Although we have appropriate ceremonies for important events, we do not consider them sacraments.

8   THE UNITARIAN UNIVERSALIST MINISTER

Q. What is a UU's concept of heaven?

*A. A **discussion** about heaven.*

How are UU ministers educated?

To be an accredited UU minister, a man or woman first must be approved by the UUA's Ministerial Fellowship Committee. This is the body which appraises the credentials and abilities of prospective ministers. A candidate must have earned an undergraduate degree and a Master of Divinity degree or higher degree from an accredited theological seminary.

Specific ministerial training is offered at Starr King School for the Ministry in Berkeley, California; Meadeville Lombard Theological School in Chicago; and the Harvard Divinity School. (Harvard Divinity School educates ministers from a number of other denominations as well.) However, a degree from any accredited theological school is acceptable, provided the candidate has specific education in Unitarian Universalism.

How do UU churches choose a minister?

When a vacancy occurs, the local church, fellowship or society appoints a Search Committee of church members. The role of the UUA at this point is to help put the Search Committee in contact with approved prospective ministers. The Committee then screens, interviews and makes its recommendations to the membership, a procedure which usually takes a year. At a special meeting the church members hear the report of the Search Committee and vote to either accept or reject the recommendation of the Search Committee.

Are there UU ministers who have entered the ministry from a non-Christian background?

Yes. They come from Christian denominations, Judaism and other faiths. While no statistics are available on the religious and philosophical backgrounds of our ministers, most have come from the Christian tradition.

What role does the minister play?

Like leaders in other religions, the minister is a teacher, guide, preacher, counselor and administrator. The minister is expected to speak the truth as he or she has come to know it, and to share that with the congregation with the understanding that members are to make up their own minds on the subject at hand.

Do ministers of different churches espouse different beliefs?

Yes, freedom of belief extends to our ministers as it does to each member. Beyond his individual beliefs, however, the minister provides as best he can, an open and accepting attitude for persons with beliefs different than his.

Can a woman be a minister in the UU church?

Yes. As a matter of fact, the Universalist Church of America was the first religion to sanction a woman minister, Olympia Brown who was ordained in 1863.

What percent of active UU ministers are women?

     53% are female and 47% are male.

What percent of those preparing for ministry are women?

     Two thirds are women.

THE UNITARIAN UNIVERSALIST CHURCH

In the early 19th century, how did the opponents of Unitarianism dismiss the religion?

"The Unitarians believe in the fatherhood of God, the brotherhood of man and the neighborhood of Boston."

Is there a head of the church?

In the traditional sense there is no individual who rules over UUs. We do elect a president of the UUA to manage the organization, to represent the UUA in the religious world and to provide a general sense of direction to its members.

If most UUs do not believe in a personal God, why are the congregations called churches?

The term God is meaningful for many of us, but we have no creed that defines this belief. Since many of our congregations were founded when Unitarianism and Universalism were liberal Christian religions, they were called churches at the time of their forming. Most still use the designation in a broader, more inclusive sense. "Church" however is not the only term used to identify a UU congregation; some are called fellowships, others societies.

Do congregations reflect America's social and racial diversity?

The process of breaking through certain demographic barriers is one of the greatest challenges to contemporary UUs. While professing to include all people, we remain a largely white, college-educated, reasonably affluent denomination. Although some of our congregations reflect a strong racial and ethnic mix, they are the exception. This is an issue with which we continue to struggle.

Do positions of leadership in UU congregations and in the UUA reflect or favor a particular religious background?

No. The leadership of a particular congregation will most likely reflect the religious makeup of that congregation, be it humanist, theist or Christian. There is no religious test for leadership positions in the UUA, only that the person be qualified for the position and have a commitment to liberal religion.

What do members do to reach out to organizations and groups in their community?

UUs have a reputation for being involved in community and civic groups and often serve on boards of human service organizations. Many churches offer their facilities to area groups who seek meeting space, such as recovery groups, community workshops and support groups.

What do children learn and study in Sunday School?

The goal of our religious program is to provide children and young people with knowledge and experiences which will help them make informed choices about their religious life as they approach adulthood.

Major goals are to teach respect for oneself and for others, appreciation of the teachings of world religious traditions, concern for social justice, and respect for our planet Earth.

Visiting other churches, they learn what various religions teach about some of life's great questions in a way appropriate for their age level.

Programs are age-appropriate from preschool through high school. For example, we have a much acclaimed course called "Our Whole Lives" for boys and girls of junior high age This course was developed jointly with the United Church of Christ (UUC), which uses the same curriculum..

10 STATISTICS

A fellowship purchased a building from a local Episcopalian congregation. After they moved in, the fellowship hung a curtain over an open space behind the altar to create a feeling of intimacy in their meetings.

Soon they decided to lay a new floor in the social hall, requiring the removal of all furniture on the floor. They moved their coffee urn into the space in back of the curtain.

A few days later, an Episcopalian work party returned to pick up some equipment they'd left behind.

Peeking behind the newly hung curtain, one of the workers immediately exclaimed, "Look here, it's true. They DO worship a coffee pot!"

from Building Your Own Theology
by Rev. Richard Gilbert

How many UUs are there?

There are 218,000 in the United States and Canada, 80,000 in Rumania, 25,000 in Hungary, and 10,000 in Great Britain and western Europe. There are small groups in India, the Philippines, and Nigeria.

Is membership growing or declining?

From the 1961 merger until the late 1970s, membership went through a slow decline similar to that of other churches. In the last four years, adult membership has shown modest growth.

*How does the growth in membership
compare to the growth of mainline
Protestant churches?*

UU membership has increased about three to four percent annually since 1986. During that same period membership in many mainline Protestant churches is down.

*How does the growth in Sunday School
enrollment compare to that of Protestant
churches?*

Since 1980, enrollment in our Sunday schools is up 40 percent; in Protestant churches it is down about 50 percent.

*What percentage of members are people
with little experience in attending Sunday
School or church services?*

Although no statistics are available, UUA's Department of Extension reports that more and more of our new members are people with little or no prior religious affiliation.

Are UUs hard to find?

Sort of. Only one American in every 1,400 is a Unitarian Universalist.

11 THE SERVICE

How important do members consider the conversations at the coffee hour following the service?

It's a toss-up which is more important— the church service or the coffee hour.

What is a typical Sunday church service like?

Our typical service follows a Protestant structure: hymms, readings, singing by the choir, organ or piano music, meditation and sermon. Most services begin with a chalice lighting (see page 32). Many have a "Sharing of Joys and Concerns" at which members speak of their personal joys, milestones, concerns and sorrows. Though the words spoken prior to the meditation might sound like a prayer, they are not addressed to a Supreme Being. The extent you would hear references to God and Jesus will depend upon the religious orientation of the particular congregation.

What symbols do you display in your churches?

In the sanctuary of most UU churches, you will find no traditional signs or symbols. However, in those churches which have chosen to retain their liberal Christian identity, you may see a cross, open Bible, or some other Christian symbol. A few churches display Christian symbols for historic purposes only.

Other churches, demonstrating their belief that there is wisdom in each of the world's religions, display symbols of many faiths: Christian, Judaism, Islam, Eastern, Native American, and others.

There are no rules laid down by our Association as to what constitutes the appropriate use of religious symbols; the decision is left to the local congregation.

What is the significance of the flaming chalice?

In the days preceding Word War II, the Boston-based Unitarian Service Committee was attempting to rescue Unitarians and other religious liberals from those parts of Europe (notably Czechoslovakia) where their lives were threatened by Naziism. The flaming chalice was the code by which those needing to be rescued identified themselves to the Unitarian Service Committee.

This symbol, which came into widespread use in Sunday services during the last 25 years, is usually lit at the beginning of the service, accompanied by a simple spoken ritual.

In our services today the chalice symbolizes wisdom, knowledge, and spiritual insight, and the flame that rises from the chalice represents the light of illumination and understanding.

What is the Flower Communion?

Many congregations observe this simple ritual in the late spring. On Flower Sunday, each person brings a flower and places it in the same large basket. At the close of the service, each person walks by the basket and removes a flower.

The variety of flowers symbolizes the variety of people, beliefs and ideas found in the congregation. Bringing a flower symbolizes the idea that each person brings something of themselves and contributes it to the service. The removal of the flower represents each person taking something away which the others have contributed.

Like the flaming chalice, this service also originated in Czechoslovakia before World War II. It was started by Czech minister Norbet

Kapek who, in Prague, was the minister of the world's largest Universalist congregation during the 1920s. and 1930s. Captured by the Nazis, he was executed at the Dachau concentration camp. His wife, Maya, who escaped to America with the help of the Service Committee, introduced the Flower Communion to congregations in the United States and Canada.

What is the extent of ritual in the church?

Unitarians and Universalists emerged from the radical free church wing of the Protestant Reformation where all types of religious ritual and liturgy were suspect. Still retaining some of that suspicion, we avoid rote ceremony or ritual for its own sake. Although we attempt to make meaningful those rituals and symbols we do use, we don't wish them to become ends in themselves.

12 JOINING THE CHURCH

A Congregational minister in a small Vermont town was asked to officiate at the funeral of an atheist, whose widow was a devout member of the local Congregational Church. Because of the deceased husband's militant atheistic views, the minister refused to conduct the service. So the local Universalist minister was enlisted to perform the funeral.

A few months later, the Congregational minister was visiting the cemetery and noticed a marker on the atheist's grave. It read, "I believe in God the Father, God the Son and God the Holy Ghost."

The minister complained to the widow, "This is ridiculous! Your husband made a career of being an atheist. Since he didn't even believe in God, he certainly didn't believe in God the Father, God the Son and God the Holy Ghost!"

The widow smiled, "Well, he does NOW!"

Can anyone be a Unitarian Universalist?

People of all beliefs are welcome to our church — Christian, atheist, agnostic, and all other traditions. What binds us as a congregation is mutual respect, acceptance of one another, and encouragement in spiritual growth.

Would an atheist be welcome and made to feel comfortable? How about agnostics, Christians, Jews, Catholics, blacks, gays, or minorities?

All of the above are welcome in any of our churches. We try to offer a place for all people regardless of where they may be on life's journey.

We affirm the inherent dignity and worth of all persons and this affirmation clearly extends to those whose sexual orientation is gay, lesbian or bisexual. Unitarian Universalism is one of the few denominations in North America that will ordain gay and lesbian clergy. The ratio of heterosexual to homosexual members in our denomination is reflective of the general population.

How actively do you try to convert people?

In the general sense of the term, we do not try to convert people at all. If people are happy and secure in their own religion, we certainly do not try to change them.

We offer an alternative for those who seek a religious home and feel they do not fit in with traditional churches.

Why do people become UUs?

About 80 percent of today's members grew up in a faith other than Unitarian Universalism. Many people who join were raised in a particular religion but in late adolescence or early adulthood became disaffected with it and stayed away from all religious involvement until they married and had children. At that time they wanted their children to have some type of religious involvement, or they themselves felt a need for a spiritual dimension in their lives. Not comfortable returning to the religion in which they were raised, they find our church a satisfactory alternative.

Some join for social reasons, some to be with like minded people, some for intellectual stimulation, and some are seeking a supportive religion in which they can pursue their own spiritual journey.

Are more people changing to Unitarian Universalism than to other religions?

In sheer numbers, no, but about 80 percent of our members have come from other faiths.

How might a person benefit by becoming a member?

If people are seeking a place where they may freely pursue their own religious, philosophical and social life journey, then they very might want to join a UU church. We like to think that in every congregation a new member will find goodwill and fellowship, plus numerous opportunities to participate.

Do most people join the church as adults?

Yes, most of today's members joined a church as an adult. Only 20 percent of our members were born into a UU family.

When people decide to join your church, what role does the church of their parents play in their decision?

When they seek a church for themselves, people may take into consideration the religious affiliation of their parents, but that usually is not the determining factor.

Is it common for people who are looking for a suitable religious community to explore a variety of possibilities by visiting several churches before making a decision?

People inquiring into Unitarian Universalism are often doing just this. They are looking for a congregagion whose beliefs, values, and practices are in synch with their own, and that meets their needs.

What are members required to do?

Although we have no participation requirements such as attending a minimum number of Sunday services, we do encourage members to take part in the activities of the congregation as their time and energy permit. To become a member you sign the membership book of that church, indicating you are in accord with the goals of UU. To become a voting member you are required to make an annual contribution to the church.

Are members expected to contribute financially to the church?

To secure financial support for their budget, most congregations conduct an annual pledge drive in which the amount of the pledge is determined by each person or family making the pledge. Many congregations offer "suggested share" guidelines based on a member's income, family size and other factors.

13 | TAKING A POSITION

Why did Rev. Theodore Parker, the most popular preacher in Boston in his time, write his sermons with a pistol by his side?

An abolitionist, he kept a pistol by his side not to protect himself, but to defend escaped slaves who were traveling the underground railroad to Canada.

Does the church take a position on public issues?

Each year at the General Assembly of the UUA, the 2,500 to 3,000 delegates vote on three or four resolutions relevant to current social, economic or environmental concerns. While the vote on these resolutions is not intended to represent every church member's opinion, it does give a broad view of UU opinion and serves to urge individual UUs to educate themselves on such matters and become involved at the local level.

Both individual ministers and lay persons often take a position as UUs on controversial public policies. Even though we make collective statements and urge specific actions, we believe that each individual must decide his or her position on every issue.

On what public issues has the church taken a position?

Recent issues include: same sex marriage, abortion, clean sources of energy, fossil fuels, energy conservation, pollution, gun control, immigration, hunger, the homeless, racism, nuclear arms proliferation, economic justice, and health care.

How active are UUs on social issues?

While it's true that those most vulnerable to injustice in our society — the poor and the minorities — are not found in great numbers in the our ranks, many individual UUs are at the forefront of social justice issues. In addition, most churches regularly give their institutional support to many social justice causes.

Although we could hardly be considered a religion of the oppressed, we cannot be fairly criticized as George Templeton Strong said of many 19th century Unitarians, most of them members of New England's privileged class: "They are sensible, plausible, candid, subtle and original in discussing any social evil or abuse. But somehow they don't get at it!"

Today, we do get at it.

What is a "Welcoming Congregation?"

The 1989 General Assembly developed a program for churches that wished to declare that they welcome gays, lesbians, bi-sexuals and transgendered persons. The program requires 12-18 months of study before the members vote. Over 400 UU congregations have voted themselves to be a Welcoming Congregation. Since the mid 1980s many UU ministers have conducted "Services of Union" ceremonies for same-sex couples who wish to make an expression of their commitment to each other, and many UU ministers are also on record as supporting the same-sex legal marriages.

What is the church's view on abortion?

As an institution, we are strongly pro-choice, as are most individual UUs.

14   UNITARIAN UNIVERSALIST LEADERS

Who said, "The Universalists believe that God is too good to damn them, and the Unitarians believe they are too good to be damned!"?

THOMAS STARR KING, *pastor of the San Francisco Unitarian Church at the start of the Civil War. Many historians credit him with saving California for the Union.*

Who are some well-known UUs?

Four United States presidents were Unitarians: **John Adams**, **John Quincy Adams**, **Millard Fillmore and William Taft**. **Thomas Jefferson** identified himself as a Unitarian, but was never a member of a Unitarian congregation as none existed in Charlottesville, Virginia. **Abraham Lincoln** had Universalist leanings but never formally joined a religious congregation of any kind.

Other well-known UUs are listed below.
- **Margot Adler**. Commentator on National Public Radio.
- **Horatio Alger** (1832-1899). Writer of rags-to-riches books for boys.
- **Conrad Aiken**. Poet and novelist.
- **Louisa May Alcott** (1832-1888). Author of *Little Women* and other books.
- **Ralph Alpher**, Physicist who developed the "big bang" model of the universe in 1948.

- **Tom Andrews**, U.S. Representative from Maine, 1991-1995.
- **Susan B. Anthony** (1820-1906. Organizer of the women's suffrage movement.
- **Adin Ballou** (1803-1890). Critic of the injustices of capitalism.
- **George Bancroft** (1800-1891), founder of the U.S. Naval Academy.
- **P. T. Barnum** (1810-1891) Well known showman, owner of the Barnum and Bailey Circus, and generous benefactor to Tufts University, founded by Universalists.
- **Béla Bartók** (1881-1945). Hungarian composer.
- **Clara Barton** (1821-1912). Founder of the American Red Cross.
- **Alexander Graham Bell** (1847-1922). Inventor of the telephone; founder of Bell Telephone Company.
- **Henry Bergh** (1811-1888), a founder of the American Society for the Prevention of Cruelty to Children.
- **Ambrose Bierce** (1842-1914).Early twentieth century writer of Civil War stories. Disappeared attempting to join Pancho Villa's revolutionary army in Mexico.
- **Charlie Bird**. One of the top guitarists of the twentieth century.
- **Nathaniel Bowditch** (1773-1838). Mathematician, navigator, astronomer.
- **Ray Bradbury**. Science fiction writer.
- **William Cullen Bryant** (1794-1878). Author and newspaper editor.
- **Charles Bulfinch** (1763-1844). Architect of the United States Capitol building.
- **Luther Burbank** (1849-1926). American botanist of the early twentieth century.
- **Robert Burns** (1759-1796), Scottish poet and song writer.
- **Rachel Carson** (1907-1964). Author of *Silent Spring* (1962), which condemned the indiscriminate use of pesticides, especially DDT.
- **William Ellery Channing** (1780-1842). Abolitionist, founder of Unitarianism in America.
- **William Cohen**. Former U. S. Senator from Maine and Secretary of Defense during the Clinton administration.
- **Norman Cousins (1915-1990)**. Humanitarian, author and editor of the *Saturday Review of Literature*. In "Anatomy of an Illness" he described how he drew on laughter to overcome a near fatal illness.

- **Nathaniel Currier** (1813-1888). Lithographer, partner of James Merritt Ives.
- **e.e. cummings** (1894-1962). Twentieth century American poet, noted for his unorthodox style and technique.
- **Clarence Darrow** (1837-1938). Attorney who argued against William Jennings Bryan in the Scopes evolution trial (1925).
- **Charles Darwin** (1809-1882). Scientist and evolutionist, author of *Origin of the Species*.
- **John Dewey** (1859-1952). Regarded as the father of progressive education in America.
- **Charles Dickens** (1812-1870), English novelist.
- **John H. Dietrich**. Humanist. Along with Curtis Reese and Charles Potter, founded the American Humanist Association in 1933.
- **Dorothea Dix** (1802-1887). Crusader for the reform of institutions for the mentally ill.
- **Don Edwards**. U.S. Representative from California for three decades.
- **Charles William Eliot** (1834-1926). President of Harvard, editor of the *Harvard Classics*.
- **Ralph Waldo Emerson** (1803-1882). Unitarian minister, philosopher, essayist.
- **Edward Everett** (1794-1865). President of Harvard, governor of Massachusetts, UU minister.
- **Fannie Farmer** (1857-1915). Cooking expert.
- **Benjamin Franklin** (1706-1790). Scientist, writer, statesman, printer.
- **Robert Fulghum**. Author of *Everything I Wanted to Know I Learned in Kindergarten* and other books.
- **Margaret Fuller** (1810-1850). A feminist before her time. Leading figure in the Transcendentalist movement and an editor of *The Dial*, along with Ralph Waldo Emerson.
- **William Lloyd Garrison** (1805-1879). Abolitionist, editor of *The Liberator*.
- **Charlotte Gilman** (1860-1935). Writer, social reformer. Major work was *Women and Economics* (1898) which focused on the need for women to gain economic independence.

- **Horace Greeley** (1811-1872). Journalist, politician, editor, and owner of the *New York Tribune,* champion of labor unions and cooperatives.
- **Edward Everett Hale** (1822-1909). Unitarian minister and author of *The Man Without a Country*.
- **Henry Hampton** (1940-1988). Writer, film-maker. Producer and director of civil rights documentary, *Eyes on the Prize*.
- **Andrew Hallidie** (1836-1900). Inventor of the cable car.
- **Frances Ellen Watkins Harper** Early twentieth century black author, poet, abolitionist, and women's rights advocate..
- **Bret Harte** (1836-1902). Writer, author of *The Luck of Roaring Camp*.
- **Nathaniel Hawthorne** (1804-1864). Nineteenth century American novelist, author of *The Scarlet Letter*.
- **John Haynes Holmes** (1879-1964). Co-founder of the American Civil Liberties Union.
- **Oliver Wendell Holmes, Jr.** (1841-1935). Lawyer and member of the U.S. Supreme Court, 1902–32.
- **Mark Hopkins** (1802-1887). Educator, theologian. Teacher of moral philosophy and later president of Williams College.
- **Julia Ward Howe** (1819-1910). Composer of *Battle Hymn of the Republic*.
- **Samuel Gridley Howe** (1801-1876). Pioneer in working with the deaf and blind.
- **Abner Kneeland** (1774-1844). Advocate of land reform, public education and birth control.
- **Lewis Lattimer** (1849-1928). African-American inventor who worked with Edison inventing numerous items associated with the light bulb.
- **Margaret Laurence** (1926-1987). Author. Her most famous books were the Manawaka series: *The Stone Angel, A Jest of God,* and others.
- **Henry Wadsworth Longfellow** (1807-1882). Poet, author of *Paul Revere's Ride*.
- **James Russell Lowell** (1819-1891). Noted nineteenth century poet, anti-slavery leader, and Unitarian minister.
- **Horace Mann** (1796-1859). A leader in the public school movement, founder of the first public school in America in Lexington, Mass; President of Antioch College; U.S. Congressman.

- **John Marshall** (1755-1835). Chief Justice of the United States Supreme Court.
- **Thomas Masaryk** (1850-1937). The first president of Czechoslovakia (1920); proponent of democracy and social justice.
- **Herman Melville** (1819-1891). Writer, author of *Moby Dick*.
- **Chris Moore**. Founder and director of Chicago Children's Choir.
- **Samuel Morse** (1791-1872). Inventor of the telegraph and Morse Code.
- **Paul Newman**. Actor in more than 60 films. Won Academy Award for Best Actor for *The Color of Money* (1986).
- **Florence Nightingale** (1820-1910). British nurse and hospital reformer.
- **Thomas Paine** (1737-1809). Editor and publisher of *Common Sense*.
- **Theodore Parker** (1810-1860). A renegade Unitarian minister of the mid-nineteenth century and a leading figure of the Abolitionist movement in the Boston area.
- **Linus Pauling** (1901-1994). Chemist. Won Nobel Peace Prize, 1962.
- **Beatrix Potter** (1866-1943). Author of *Peter Rabbit* and other children's stories.
- **Joseph Priestly** (1733-1804). Discoverer of oxygen, Unitarian minister.
- **Elliot Richardson** (1920-1999). Former Secretary of Health, Education and Welfare; former Attorney General (1973).
- **James Reeb**. A UU minister, he was killed at Selma, Alabama in a civil rights demonstration.
- **Paul Revere** (1735-1818). Silversmith and patriot.
- **Malvina Reynolds**. Social activist. Along with Woody Guthrie and Pete Seeger, wrote *Little Boxes*.
- **Tim Robbins**. Film actor, director, and writer. Either acted in, wrote, directed, or composed songs in *Bob Roberts, Shawshank Redemption*, and *Dead Man Walking*.
- **Benjamin Rush** (1745-1813). Signer of the Declaration of Independence; physician, considered to be the "Father of American Psychiatry."
- **Carl Sandberg** (1878-1967). Poet, writer, folklorist. Wrote *Chicago* (1914) and won Pulitzer Prize for his biography of Lincoln

- **Margaret Sanger** (1879-1966). Birth control advocate. Founded the *Birth Control Review* in 1916. Helped establish 300 doctor-staffed medical clinics. Assisted in founding Planned Parenthood.
- **May Sarton** (1912-1995). Poet, writer. Wrote *Endgame: A Journal of the Seventy-Ninth Year* (1992)
- **Pete Seeger**. Songwriter, singer, and social activist.
- **Rod Serling** (1924-1975). Television scriptwriter. Author of 200 television plays. Won six Emmy awards.
- **Robert Shaw**. Founder of Robert Shaw Chorale; assistant conductor of Cleveland Orchestra; conductor of Atlanta Symphony.
- **Ted Sorenson**. Speechwriter and aide to John F. Kennedy.
- **Charles Steinmetz** (1865-1923). Electrical engineer; holder of 200 patents; known for his theoretical studies of alternating current.
- **Adlai Stevenson** (1900-1965). Governor of Illinois; candidate for President of the United States; U.S. Ambassador to the U.N.
- **George Stephenson** (1781-1848). English engineer. Invented the first locomotive.
- **Gilbert Charles Stuart** (1755-1828). Artist. Best known for his portrait of George Washington.
- **Sylvanus Thayer** (1785-1872). Engineer. Founded U.S. Military Academy.
- **Clyde Tombaugh** (1906-1997). Astronomer. Discovered the ninth planet, Pluto.
- **Henry David Thoreau** (1817-1862). Essayist and naturalist. Author of *Walden Pond*.
- **Hendrik Wilhem Van Loon** (1882-1944). Historian and author.
- **Kurt Vonnegut**. Writer. Author of *Slaughterhouse-Five*.
- **Daniel Webster** (1782-1852). Orator; U.S. Senator; Secretary of State; candidate for President of the United States.
- **Josiah Wedgwood** (1730-1795). English potter. Founder of Wedgwood Pottery.
- **William Carlos Williams**. Physician and poet.
- **Frank Lloyd Wright** (1869-1959). Architect.
- **Owen D. Young** (1874-1962). Chairman of General Electric Company.
- **Whitney Young** (1921-1971). Head of the Urban League.

15   THE FINAL QUESTION

Why aren't there more Unitarian Universalists?

While most people turn to religion for comfort, and for answers that are beyond challenge, Unitarian Universalism challenges the person to find his or her own answers. Even on those rare occasions when it suggests an answer, our religion often insists that the person challenge, compare and weigh the proposed prescription.

In the United States, most religions are authoritative, in contrast to Unitarian Universalism which is based on reason and the individual's freedom of belief.

For most people, our religion presents an excess of freedom; many prefer someone else or some institution to provide the answers to life's mysteries.

Culturally, most Americans do not realize that Unitarian Universalism even exists. Millions pass through high school and college without ever hearing or reading about this religion, a situation made possible because most Americans recognize only three major religions: you are either Catholic, Protestant or Jewish. Unitarian Universalism, a very different way of approaching religion, is none of the above.

For these reasons, plus our aversion to proselytize, most new members are forced to "stumble" on our religion; it's a wonder that we have as many members as we do. But maybe this small publication will provide some useful information to those who might be considering an alternative to mainstream religion.